Haiku
Country

Lawrence Eyre

Haiku Country

Lawrence Eyre

Copyright © 2020 Lawrence Eyre

Published by 1st World Publishing
P.O. Box 2211, Fairfield, Iowa 52556
tel: 641-209-5000 • fax: 866-440-5234
web: www.1stworldpublishing.com

First Edition
Library of Congress Control Number: 2020935157
Softcover ISBN: 978-1-4218-3652-2

Back cover portrait by John Bakker.
Cover design by Emmy Auge.
Cover photograph Jefferson County, Iowa Conservation Board.

Introduction

Mom says life's like court
Tell the truth the whole truth and
Nothing but the truth

I love you Mom but
That's a real tall order with
So few syllables

Miss Emily wrote
Tell the truth but tell it slant
That sounds more like it

Everything's riding
On three slender rails let's go
Miss Emily's way

Haiku Country

In haiku country
Extra syllables die fast
Seventeen or bust

Haiku country rocks
Oldfangled five seven five
Three chords and the truth

My self-driving truck
Left me in the dust today
Cryin' in my beer

Haiku country's not
Just one place it's everywhere
Folks love life simple

Fly Haiku Airways
Sorry No Baggage Allowed
Please Sit In Three Rows

You are entering
Haiku country we hope you
Enjoy peace within

Yoda loves this place
Here live calm stay haiku read
Force will with you be

A while back haiku
Country beckoned silently
You will like it here

Log cabin life in
The middle of nowhere will
Suit you fine just now

When we trust water
We can dive naked into
A shining future

Deer race me sometimes
Veering off from my truck just
Before venison

In sacred places
Spirals of silence often
Rise from soil itself

Some of this may sound
Like I left my tool shed door
Unlocked way too long

That could be so but
I hope you will hear me out
Both of us may learn

Yale's Latin motto
Hinted what life could offer
Lux et Veritas

Light plus truth Yale said
One helps see the other I've
Gone all in for both

Northside snow's melting
Shovels stand at ease until
The next storm gathers

Mild winter weather
Doesn't last long we should mend
Some fences today

Geese honk donkeys bray
Elephants trumpet there are
Times I'd vote for geese

Some folks think it's sin
To say sorry nowadays
Let's just take that risk

Here's love for purple
Our own mountains' majesty
Blends the red and blue

The better angels
Of our nature love life with
Even half a loaf

Words that get thumbs-up
Here may start fights over there
Kindly silence helps

Even friendliness
May get pushback now but
Smiles win in the end

Fact is we can do
Only so many right things
In a single day

So sin boldly not
Doing right brings more regret
Than doing what's wrong

Kids all wondered why
Old people yelled at us when
We ran through their yards

Lately we've learned
Folks need a patch of peace in
An untidy world

Cold weather blasts back
But austerity is just
Challenge in these parts

Memories quicken
Here long before first light on
Stark winter mornings

Mom thanks for teaching
Letters to your lefty but
He wrote them backwards

I printed my name
In mirror writing first day
Of kindergarten

We miss you Dad but
Your brave vigilance inspires
Our stand for world peace

Dad in your honor
We still belt Broadway tunes with
Improvised wrong words

Facing a mirror
At age ten I realize
Somebody's in there

I drop the school drum
And promptly get encouraged
To join the boys' choir

Porch swings take us back
First to childhood playgrounds then
To our own cradles

The Whiffenpoofs I
Heard first night at Yale sang so
Strong I got goosebumps

A lifetime honor
Shared with gentlemen songsters
Still off on a spree

Singing never stops
Melodies move inside when
Voices go silent

USA Tennis
Coach Of The Year Moline Kid
Still Smiles Ear To Ear

Nightmare memories
Echo too though some now seem
More like miracles

I heard my head hit
The highway but thankfully
Live to tell the tale

Steel Girders Strike Road
Split Ahead of Speeding Car
Sparing Driver's Life

As the ambulance
Pulled away I realized
She might not make it

I was thrilled even
To hear snoring it meant my
Wife was still alive

Sudden virulent
Spinal meningitis swept
Laurie to the edge

Can't claim to know how
But thank God Laurie lived past
That one-hour window

Laurie squeezed my hand
Long and strong when the ordeal
Had finally passed

For two become one
Trouble may double but a
Life shared is joy squared

When one of us leaves
We talk about what counts most
You never know when

In haiku country
People speak about death with
Respect but not fear

Admittedly life
Carries death within it but
That means life's larger

Death's nearby of course
But doesn't rule in the end
Life's winner is love

Life and death revolve
Around the selfsame point deep
In realms of silence

Haiku people prize
Proverbial wisdom they
They can apply to life

Sometimes stars line up
And we have no choice but to
Stand and deliver

Silver linings may
Turn out to be worth much more
Than their weight in gold

Time for you to take
A stand they shout fine I stand
For wholeness of life

Finding enough love
Inside to go extra miles
Sometimes takes searching

We grow through challenge
Eliminating hurdles
Keeps us from jumping

Dazzling descriptions
Of the mountaintop may not
Help us scale the heights

Life at the speed of
Growing grass sends surprising
Messages our way

Decades tax our hearts
But love can mend and send them
High above time's toll

Old people retell
Stories so we remember
Not because they don't

Buoyed by memories
Happy centenarians
Float through the present

Pure simplicity
Visits often but only
Stays where all is clean

Treasured rituals
Allow our mind to settle
Toward the simple

Small slights don't seem to
Matter but they pile up and
Tip the scales of justice

Mindless keystrokes fly
Faster than the speed of thought
Toward hurts unknown

Light doesn't throw shade
Truth doesn't clap back even
When there's no applause

You know that water
Under bridges I'm not sure
All of it stays gone

Clippings said wedding
In March baby October
He could count to nine

Poetic license
Lets me write certain things I
Wouldn't say aloud

Blessings disguised as
Disaster we decode by
Unmasking ourselves

Thank you for helping
Costs nothing to say but means
Everything to hear

Looking down noses
Discloses hearts with uphill
Climbs to happiness

Shunning survivors
Rarely revisit scenes of
Their suffocation

Hard times we grow through
Are really just training for
Glory down the road

Galileo saw
Thirty-six Pleiades stars
Through his telescope

Our DNA strands
Could stretch beyond Jupiter
Who says we are small

Her fans sent letters
Because she had touched their hearts
She answered each one

He never tried to
Carve out a career but work
Came through what he loved

Plush says we've made it
Plain prods productivity
There's a middle way

In haiku and life
It helps to fill gaps with our
Imagination

Austerity's gift
Is a treasure chest full of
Free experience

Most folks spin cocoons
To wall themselves safely in
Not to shut us out

There's light that we see
And there's light by which we see
Both belong to God

God's will may grind us
Down to dust in order to
Plant seeds for new life

Life can go dark and
Gain glory at the same time
Taketh and giveth

Peace begins within
Peace moves from my team to ours
Peace unites us all

Contempt curdles our
Own blood long before it sours
The hearts of others

The stories we craft
To protect ourselves are the
Hardest to rewrite

Don't fling syllables
Into wind without watching
Where they come to rest

Scars are souvenirs
Of sorts reminders that growth
May cost us comfort

Open hearts span far
Beyond our frames scanning the
Wider world for love

Snark barks but silence
Stops a spiral of smallness
Before it can start

When milestones start to
Feel like millstones maybe it's
Time to change venues

Chapter endings call
For simple benediction
Spoken from the heart

Starlight aeons old
Somehow launches hearts ahead
To future glory

Athletes are advanced
Artists whose joy shines forth as
Wholeness on the move

It's nothing fancy
But just breathing through our nose
Calms things down a lot

Dressing in layers
Feels great and burns less bread than
Keeping homes toasty

Beatles and Beach Boys
Wrote haiku songs long before
Anyone noticed

She came in through the
Bathroom window protected
By a silver spoon

Be true to your school
Just like you would to your girl
Let your colors fly

Some people think we
Might be hard-wired for haiku
I just like the songs

Believe it or not
Roy Rogers' Happy Trails was
Meant to close Woodstock

In Bermuda on
Good Friday they fly kites to
Show us what comes next

Brother Scott now plays
Scorching lead guitar licks for
Heaven's baddest band

The clearest vision
Of what counts most in our life
May come through closed eyes

Small child asks teacher
May I hug you yes thank you
Universe applauds

We walked opposite
Directions but reached the field's
Edge at the same time

Snakes seen slithering
In shadows may prove to be
Nothing more than strings

Needless suffering
Comes from craving perfection
Where it can't be found

Grandpa Thomas Eyre
Saw Cubs win the World Series
In 1908

Dear child Nana ate
Horseradish sauce but sat in
Silence as tears streamed

They burned old car tires
One winter because all the
Coal money was gone

Great Grandma Carlson
Never drank but sure loved her
Swedish cough syrup

If a mother in
Labor craves tomatoes then
You just find her some

Art Teacher's Son Tells
Kindergarten Classmates That's
Chartreuse Not Yellow

To ancient Greeks a
Life of noble excellence
Was the shining goal

If your way supports
Life I'm for it no matter
What tribes we come from

Some say gratitude
Is attitude but thanks must
Be to be given

Unsolicited
Advice is welcomed rarely
Heeded even less

Making a virtue
Of necessity upholds
Challenged dignity

Better to rely
On diligence than to hope
For strokes of good luck

I can see why some
Old folks mutter to themselves
As they shuffle by

Taken for granted
Love dies on the vine there is
No benign neglect

The same medicine
That kills ills taken too long
Buries patients too

I've got to admit
Weeds left alone can bring us
Beautiful flowers

Shots at redemption
Withheld become cannonballs
We're forced to carry

Dancing on graves is
Often unwitting prelude
To digging our own

When we are empty
From giving all rest assured
God will grant us more

Even at zero
We can feel midwinter sun's
Growing radiance

If delight doesn't
Flow maybe compassion can
If not just don't mind

Transmuting trials
Into truth raw delta blues
Strikes lightning in souls

Land sings its own song
Lucky ones listen and add
Their best harmony

Great rivers give birth
To civilizations that
Match their character

Take a lifetime's worth
Of syllables knead into
Fresh haiku and serve

A labor of love
Demands more than a job but
Doesn't feel like work

It may take a thorn
To remove a thorn sometimes
That's how life cleans us

Poems protect hearts
In jeopardy climbing their
Way back to safety

Bones snap by themselves
They can't bend until they start
Working with neighbors

Rows harder to hoe
Than our own have already
Been plowed by others

Teeth may turn crooked
With the passage of time but
Our smiles stay honest

Lies serve as armor
Sometimes but they weigh a lot
And rust from inside

If God's on our side
When enemies fail who fails
When enemies don't

Enemies come from
Insufficient friendliness
Inside our own hearts

Triumph may be shared
Even when victory can't
Foes lift each other

The silence trailing
Our most profound questions is
Really their answer

Even routine chores
Take on quiet joy after
A narrow escape

Nature may be a
Little cruel in order
To be greatly kind

When we're sure someone
Stepped in cow pies how about
We check our boots first

In the end we see
Truth is one the wise call it
By different names

All the milk may spill
Everything may fall apart
But love still triumphs

Happy trails to you
Until we meet again keep
Smiling until then

Haiku people look
On life's lighter side even
When floods come they float

Restrictions Apply
This Offer Expires As Soon
As The Fine Print Dries

Grandma sweetly said
A new broom sweeps the floor clean
Then gave us dustpans

Life's never-ending
Battle for truth justice and
Sideburns the same length

OK Boomer is
Fair payback for wearing those
Garish bell bottoms

You'd have thought I made
Kids dig the Erie Canal
Not read about it

You can take teachers
Out of the classroom but you
Can't take the classroom

Hey Sith happens in
A galaxy far away
But teaches us here

Haiku revival
Right here in river city
Let's hear an amen

If five seven five
Patrols this space we can say
Whatever pleases

First lines just show up
Finding a great second line
May take some digging

Third lines seal the deal
When they tweak minds and lift hearts
Mission accomplished

It isn't the end
Of the world it just sounds that
Way on the news shows

What causes more harm
Ignorance or apathy
Don't know and don't care

Brilliant thoughts can shine
Through us but we may need to
Dust off dim bulbs first

Some haiku simply
Arrive with the stork others
Need longer labor

The buck doesn't stop
Deer antlers grow as much as
Half an inch per day

What does it all mean
Mr. Natural please crack
Dr. Bronner's code

I don't know many
Old folks who like to be called
Permanent fixtures

Difficult haiku
Feel like whittling bark-covered
Branches down to sticks

Grandma said don't show
Everything leave them something
To wonder about

I hope you can tell
All is well because if I
Haiku I like you

No fancy dancing
I still have trouble telling
Hay foot from straw foot

Lavish syllable
Spending quickly bankrupts a
Promising haiku

Grapes of wrath ferment
So fast now we can hear corks
Popping in Congress

I keep trying but
My mute button doesn't work
For current events

We saw a group of
Sophomores trying on fresh
Personas for size

Hearts give us over
Two and a half billion great
Beats we can dance to

Those who do not know
History are condemned to
Listen to who does

Stories told in just
Seventeen syllables tend
To be skeletal

Innumeracy
Cowers in classroom corners
That math teacher's back

Lefties rule even
Though 90% of the
World says we're not right

Incompetence thinks
It's doing great what's wrong with
All these naysayers

Eighth graders follow
Us to the earth's end if they
Don't drive us there first

In case of haiku
Attack please seek shelter in
The nearest basement

If you don't wear socks
We don't care if you don't brush
Your teeth we do care

No haiku today
Five seven five drives me nuts
Well maybe one more

Give me ellipses
I can make criminals sound
Like canonized saints

Lots of people think
Turtles are slow but they get
The shell outta here

If everybody
I meet today is a jerk
That means I'm the jerk

Commands to cease and
Desist will meet with cheerful
Noncompliance here

Geezer coach wheezes
Wisdom the older we get
The better we were

It's pretty hard to
Get stressed out over haiku
But some folks manage

Time to dance varmint
Tap out them syllables or
Firin' will commence

Save on Christmas gifts
Talk politics at your feast
On Thanksgiving Day

We're pleased to report
Sun moon and stars are still in
Their usual spots

Get Off My Cornfield
Cantankerous Iowa
Farmer Turns 90

Your future can be
Virtually assured just
Trust in your selfie

Seriously folks
If laughter helps health the joke
Is in us not on

Counting syllables
Sure beats counting calories
Pass the apple pie

Great tasting haiku
Deliver knowledge nuggets
That melt in your mind

Old Haiku Country
Gent Writes Life Lessons Before
He Forgets Them All

OK I'm old in
Fahrenheit but Celsius
Says I'm 21

Old new borrowed blue
Something for everybody
All are welcome here

For fun I stretch some
Haiku into one line and
Write real sentences

When it snows before
Halloween people bewitch
About cold for months

Grammar Explodes Shards
Loll Shamelessly While Police
Haul Haiku To Court

Lose touch with bedrock
As soon as we start taking
This life for granite

We get seventeen
Syllables around here pal
Your meter's running

Go ahead make my
Haiku do you feel lucky
Gentle grasshopper

Balding geezers may
Still see consummate studs in
The shaving mirror

Folks who can't decide
To fish or cut bait live in
A big can of worms

Hardly a driver
Now alive who passed on hills
At 75

Silence is golden
Whispering wind is silver
Geese are God's brass band

Even the choir can
Start calling in sick if we
Do too much preaching

There's no denying
Major mileage but we've still
Got plenty of tread

Did someone order
Two nothingburgers minus
The mayo to go

Far be it from me
To tell people what to eat
May your food taste great

We kept on truckin'
We kept it real now we just
Keep forgetting things

Build a kinder world
Seventeen syllables at
A time buy haiku

Haiku people love
Nature's quiet beauty and
Rich simplicity

In seeming homage
Heaven's highest clouds parted
For tonight's full moon

Night utterly still
But for crickets chirping at
An old gibbous moon

Green turned gold last night
As exhaled freshness floated
To the firmament

The deep sweetness in
Haiku country air begins
In our own silence

The graceful arcs of
A squirrel's tail match its leaps
Along forest floors

Our clouds' undersides
Blushed pink at sunset but soon
Regained composure

We think dragonflies
Are the greatest they feast on
Mosquitoes full time

Two rumpled old ducks
Warm themselves roadside while there's
Still enough sunshine

Windswept white dunes cast
Unearthly shadows in late
December daylight

On warm winter days
The land yawns stretches a bit
Then goes back to sleep

Moon slice above dawn's
Palette winks knowingly while
We're left to wonder

A circle of soft
Gosling feathers was all the
Foxes left behind

Muted moonbeams stretch
Toward dusty galaxies
In Debussy sky

Birds sing spring songs on
This mild Christmas morning all
Is calm all is bright

Huge noctilucent
Clouds herald a season of
Heavenly vision

Loons on lake echo
Each other fluting welcome
Or warning to all

Moonlight dances down
From prairie skies across lakes
And straight into hearts

Sun rises over
Ground fog turning this valley's
Vapor into gold

A bald eagle flies
Across our windshield into
Deep orange sunset

Dawn's early light fades
Dimming distant hay fields and
Drawing minds inside

Haiku country moon
Lights the way home on roads we've
Always known by heart

A green acorn falls
In lakeside breeze denting pine
Needles without sound

The air is filled with
Strenuous objection honked
By geese flying cold

Dashing through the snow
Deer freeze at the sight of kids'
Halloween costumes

Flying as fractals
Flocks of tiny birds swoop in
And out of our lives

Turkey vultures sit
Atop an abandoned house
Scanning for supper

Shadows flee on foot
At light's stealth arrival while
Wind awaits the news

Eight-point buck on the
Hillside casts a long shadow
In low-slung sunlight

How often do we
See a sunset's glory straight
Through steady downpour

At the confluence
Of sacred streams even mist
Is filled with blessing

Degrees drop sharply
But harvest farmscapes fill hearts
With summer's stored warmth

Ice from yesterday's
Puddle stares back blankly this
December morning

Ghostly cornstalks stand
Bleached in winter sun waiting
For the reaper's blade

Plastering trees with
Flung snowballs is excellent
Winter therapy

Full moon's tranquil beams
Fill this frozen lake with an
Undiminished glow

One straggling gaggle
Of geese huddles lakeside to
Plot their escape route

Last geese left today
Some say low solar angle
Maybe it's just cold

High wedges wend south
Above Father of Waters'
Lustrous silver band

Tonight's full moon shines
Soft on weather-beaten land
Mending in silence

Iowa's dusted
With confectioner's sugar
Ready for breakfast

Late winter sun seems
Content to send muted light
Time is on its side

Demure dawn can't stop
This howling wind but take heart
Warmth is on the way

Gold shafts burst through seams
Of thick eastern grey there will
Be light this morning

Life leans toward spring
Again and again fields thaw
And we plow fresh ground

Butterflies dance in
Silence but I'd swear I hear
Fugue in A Major

Cornrows in contoured
Fields curve into the distance
Pulling our minds home

Rainbow bends above
Iowa fields blessing the
Bounty beneath it

About the Author

Born in Iowa
Along the Mississippi
Where the steamboats push

Great-grandfather farmed
Grandpa and Dad worked for Deere
I teach what I've learned

Yale's yes plus fifty
Years back home ripened me to
Write *Heartland Haiku* (2019)

CPSIA information can be obtained
at www.ICGtesting.com
Printed in the USA
FSHW010403270320
68519FS